How to Affirm Success
On The Way To Your Dreams

by Sheree L. Ross
Copyright © 2023

DISCLAIMER

First Edition

BOOKS

Affirming Life: A Daily Meditation

Affirming Business: For Career and Entrepreneurial Excellence

"Fulfillment isn't found over the rainbow—

it's found in the here and now.

Today I define success by the fluidity

with which I transcend emotional

land mines and choose joy

and gratitude instead."

RuPaul Charles

INTRODUCTION

I believe that we all deserve levels of success in our lives so it's important to recognize that everyone has the potential to achieve it in their own unique way. Success can be defined in many different ways and it can look different for every person, so as we go on this journey together I want you to carry the knowledge that you have more control over your reality than you think. In fact, your thoughts can have a profound effect on your reality. If you consistently think negative thoughts, you are much more likely to experience negative events in your reality. On the flip side, if you place your focus on more positive thoughts and visualizations you are more likely to align with a more positive reality. With that said, it is also true that the world has been in an awakening for many decades but there was also a significant quickening after the Covid-19 outbreak, as well as the racial, economic and civil unrest that continue to unfold This quickening has affected all of our lives in different ways and as you adapt and adjust to these new energies remember to be kind to yourself and know that we all come to our understandings in our own time.

Big changes create new ways of seeing the world and many of us are re-defining how we view success. During the 2020 quarantine a new paradigm was set in motion around work and success. Our priorities changed and many of us were snapped out of a lifetime of following lockstep in the *'work hard, get promoted, buy more stuff until retirement or death'* mentality. We have been trained to know that the old paradigm of success is status and money, but now we are finding that the awakened mind is calling for broader definitions. The tried and true definition of wealth and power will always be defined in terms of money, but to someone who defines success as people it could mean having a big family or lots of friends. To someone else who defines it as achievement they might climb a mountain or own a business. The great news is, however you define it, your definition is as important and valuable as anyone else's.

So how do we get started on this journey towards success? Well the first and most important step is for you to have complete clarity on the goals you want to achieve. Without a clear set of goals you will not know if you are on the right track, you will not have a measure of your achievements, and you will not be able to understand when you are being guided by your inner voice to take certain steps. Many people think that it is enough to just want to be successful, but the Universe does not dictate your existence. Even on the most spiritual level - releasing and letting God - you first have to decide to do so. I recommend taking some time right now or when you have some moments alone and set some dynamic and exciting goals. I say dynamic and exciting because goals like "do the dishes" or "get the car maintenanced" are not what I have in mind. Creating goals that make you stretch in all areas of your life bring an exciting energy that will help you stay engaged when the going gets tough. If you've ever wanted to own a sports car, research which kind and put that on your list. If you want to go back to school and get an advanced degree, put that on your list. Don't limit yourself because you have no idea how you are going to be able to take the time, or find the money to do it. Just dream and let the ideas flow. Write them down so that you can review them daily, and then come back to this book and continue on your journey towards your life's dreams.

Now that you are clear on your goals, the next step is to remember that we create what we focus on and our number one focusing tool are our thoughts, especially thoughts that we focus on repeatedly. What you focus on and what you think about all day creates how you feel. Feelings are vibrations, and what you energetically vibrate to is what you align with in your reality. Put another way, the reason you feel the way that you do is because of the way you think. The reason things keep appearing in your life is because of the way you feel. If you think the world is for or against you, you will feel a certain way about it, and this creates a vibration that aligns you with the reality of that thought. Ultimately, the world around you is a mirror, reflecting back to you how you feel. To be a metaphysical master is to understand that it's never the other person and not really even the overall circumstances. These people and events are just reflecting back to you the energy you are putting out at any given moment.

You can change any interaction, circumstance, even your current reality just by taking the time to change your inner reality. The process looks like this - your thoughts become beliefs, solidifying your vibration point, and your beliefs soon become your way of vibrating in the world; habits of conditioning are then formed and your life vibrates to what you believe is the result of something happening outside of you. Understanding the alignment process is tantamount to creating the practice necessary to change the habits that will give you the results of success you seek. Not knowing will have you believing that you don't have the power to change your life, when in truth, life is a reflection of repetitive thinking and narrowed focus on things that don't bring you the life you want. The good news is, we are all pretty practiced already at repetitive and narrowed thinking, now you get to do it with purpose.

Now that you have your new clarity and intentional focus, you are on your way to creating new beliefs, new feelings, new energy, and thus new outcomes. In fact, you will be able to gauge where you are on the spectrum of alignment based on how you are feeling at any point during the day. If you are feeling glum or worried, observe what you've been thinking and focused on. Have you been watching the news? Have you focused for long periods of time on what's not working in your life? This is not to say that if you have something that needs your attention that you should ignore it. What I am saying is that you need to balance all of the day-to-day with as much positive and affirmative intake as you do the opposite so you can move your vibration closer to your end goals.

So now that you have achieved clarity and are on the path towards change, where do affirmations fit into all of this? Affirmations can be used to observe the responses in your mind and body as you say them. Doing this is a great way to use the tool of affirmations. Observing yourself is one of the easiest ways to change your behavior and your thinking. At first you will feel resistance, this is normal, it is also a great indicator that something about that affirmation isn't vibrating with you in your belief system. This might be the belief that is preventing you from moving forward. Affirmations that trigger a resistant feeling need to be better understood so don't just say affirmations for the sake of saying them without observing whether or not you are able to fully take on board what they are affirming.

It doesn't matter whether or not the affirmation is stating something that is absolutely true in your life at this moment, what will matter is whether or not you honestly believe it can happen or that it is in the process of happening for you. The beliefs and thoughts that you have that are blocking your efforts will be brought into the light if you will take the time to observe and write down what you are feeling. Meditate on these feelings. Journal about them and if you feel comfortable doing so, write out affirmations that support the new outcome that you want to feel. You will know you are moving on when you can say the affirmation and experience little to no resistance at all.

You are now becoming more like the

energy of the success you seek!

As most of us know, like attracts like. This is a simplified vibrational understanding of how the universe works. We don't really manifest our desires, it's more like we attract or align with them. In other words, you must get up to speed with the energy of the success you are seeking in order to align with its outcome. That is the purpose of affirmations. Not to attract. Not to create out of the atmosphere like magic. They are used as a focusing tool to help you get your energy and emotions up to the vibration of your desires. The mind is a powerful tool and once you harness the understanding of how to use it you will have a different outer reality. Repetition is the mother of skill. The more you do the affirmations in this book and ones that you create on your own, the more your mind will take on the new information and your vibration will shift.

There are three sections in this book. A question section where I will prompt you with questions that I encourage you to take the time to answer to help get clarity and begin to build momentum. An affirmation section where I have created affirming statements to be used daily to help you recalibrate your vibrational field and move into alignment with your goals. And by the way, it's okay if you don't believe what you are affirming in the beginning. Very few of us do. This isn't about conjuring up success. It

is about changing you at a core level so that you align with success. If you can only say

these affirmation with the idea that "wouldn't it be nice if..." then try that. One of these

days, if you do them long enough, you will find that something inside of you changes

and you'll feel more and more confident in making the statement. Then there is a

gratitude section, there is no faster way to change your point of view and vibrational

stance than by placing your focus on the things in your life that you appreciate and are

grateful for on a daily basis. I would highly recommend starting a gratitude journal that

you use both in the morning and right before you go to bed. In fact, if the only thing you

get from this book is to look around for things to be grateful for all day and do that for

30 days you will more than likely find that you are happier, more hopeful, and that your

life is already improving in many areas.

"Successful people ask better questions,

and as a result, they get better answers."

Tony Robbins

ASKING BETTER

AND

BETTER QUESTIONS

CLARITY IS KEY

So, what is the big deal about asking yourself questions? Good question! Asking yourself thoughtful and deliberate questions helps shift your focus towards your desired goal. Learning how to ask yourself better questions will improve your life in ways you will begin to experience over time if you make it a practice. It can allow you to gain different perspectives and this process will ultimately allow you to make better choices. The key to asking yourself questions is to understand that not just any old question will do. The goal is to go deeper and break through the layers of lack of clarity with each one so the better the quality of the question the better the quality of the answer. Of course, great answers don't do us any good without action. You must take action on the answers you receive and this combination leads to more successes in life.

Another key to using questions is to not ask the same set of questions over and over again, assuming your inner voice isn't giving you answers. Also, asking yourself challenging questions, introspective questions, results-oriented questions can make a huge difference in the results you get. After asking, take time to *LISTEN* with an open mind and heart. Listen to the feelings that come up and your instincts to take action, these are some of the ways that you receive answers. If the answers scare you, that's okay. Just jot them down and sit with them awhile. Sometimes the answers may seem opaque so you may need to meditate in order to really hear what's being said. Sometimes the answers might make you feel uncomfortable, but don't ignore them. Be patient with yourself during this time and know that the Universe will give you the answer as often as you need in as many iterations as needed for you to finally hear it, embody it, embrace it, and then take action on it.

Knowing how to ask yourself better and better questions, in order to get better and better answers, is a great way to move the needle of understanding on what steps to take and how to go about them. As usual, you must begin with a clear end result in mind. What is it that you want to achieve or understand? This helps you create more focused and insightful questions that are empowering and help you focus on solutions rather than problems. "How do I achieve xyz?" vs "Why isn't this working?" Also, don't bombard your consciousness with lots of questions all at once. You are really doing this to get clear and actionable answers so be patient, deliberate, and ask them one at a time, truly seeking clear answers. Get clear on which questions are important in order to take the steps necessary to achieve your goal. Below, find some starter questions, answer these and then create your own set of better questions that really needle down to the answers you are seeking. Remember to listen for the answers and then take actions when inspired to do so.

QUESTIONS

- What does success mean to me?

- What does my successful life look like in every area; health, money, business, career, relationships, spirituality, etc.?

- What do I need to do more of in order to achieve my goals?

- What do I need to do less of in order to achieve my goals?

- What are five steps I can take right now to help me towards my goal?

- In what areas do I need to ask for help?

- Who has the kind of success that I want?

- What skills and habits do they have that I need to make a part of my process?

- What are my moving towards values?

- What are my moving away from values?

- What does success feel like to me?

- What does success look like to me?

- What success have I achieved in the past?

- What are five of my personal goals?

- What are five of my career goals?

- What are five of my business goals?

- What are my income goals?

- What are my investment goals?

- What are my relationship goals?

- What are my health goals?

- What are my spiritual goals?

- What are my creative goals?

- What are my giving goals?

- What are my family goals?

- What are ten things that I am grateful for?

- What do I need to do in order to prepare myself to receive my intentions?

- Am I taking the time each day to do the steps necessary? If not, how can I become consistent?

- As I take measure, what new experiences am I having that show me I'm on the right track?

- What are the things that I need to add to my daily steps?

- What are the things that that I need to change in order to achieve my goals?

- How can I help someone else on their journey of success?

"Success is liking yourself,

liking what you do,

and liking how you do it."

Maya Angelou

AFFIRMATIONS

I make measure of my progress

on a daily basis.

I apply the guidance

coming to me and reap

the success I intend.

I have a clear picture now.

I am clear on what it means

for me to be successful and

I am excited to align with it.

I love what I do,

I love where I am in this process,

I give thanks for this journey.

I make an effort everyday

to feel what it is that makes

me feel successful.

I make an effort everyday

to dream my dreams

and visualize what

success looks like for me.

I love what I do.

I am so thankful that I am very successful.

I appreciate the loving

relationships in my life.

I carry the energy of

my success with me all day...everyday,

and give thanks that things in my

life are always working out for me

with joy and ease.

By affirming what I want every day I am

making sure my journey is as

positive, joyful, and direct as possible.

I am that! I am.

I am that success.

I am that intention.

I am that desire.

I am that dream.

I keep the faith.

I do not waiver.

I let go and let the powers of

the Universe unfold my journey.

I am so grateful for my health and

do what is necessary to continue

to create great synergy

in my body, mind, spirit.

I am worth the money I am asking for!

I am becoming more in tune, more powerful,

and more empowered everyday.

I am delighted as

the momentum of good things

unfold in my life, every day.

Joy follows me throughout my day.

I take time to understand my intention/s,

then take the time to understand my blocks

and replace those thoughts and beliefs.

I reset my focus every morning

by rereading my intentions and

asking the Universe what it is I

need to do to align

with my ultimate desire.

I actively seek to

illuminate and eliminate

the limitations in my mind

and clear resistance

in my energy field.

I know I'm on my way

to bigger and better things.

What is it that I need to do today

to bring me closer to my intentions?

Life is working out for me in every way.

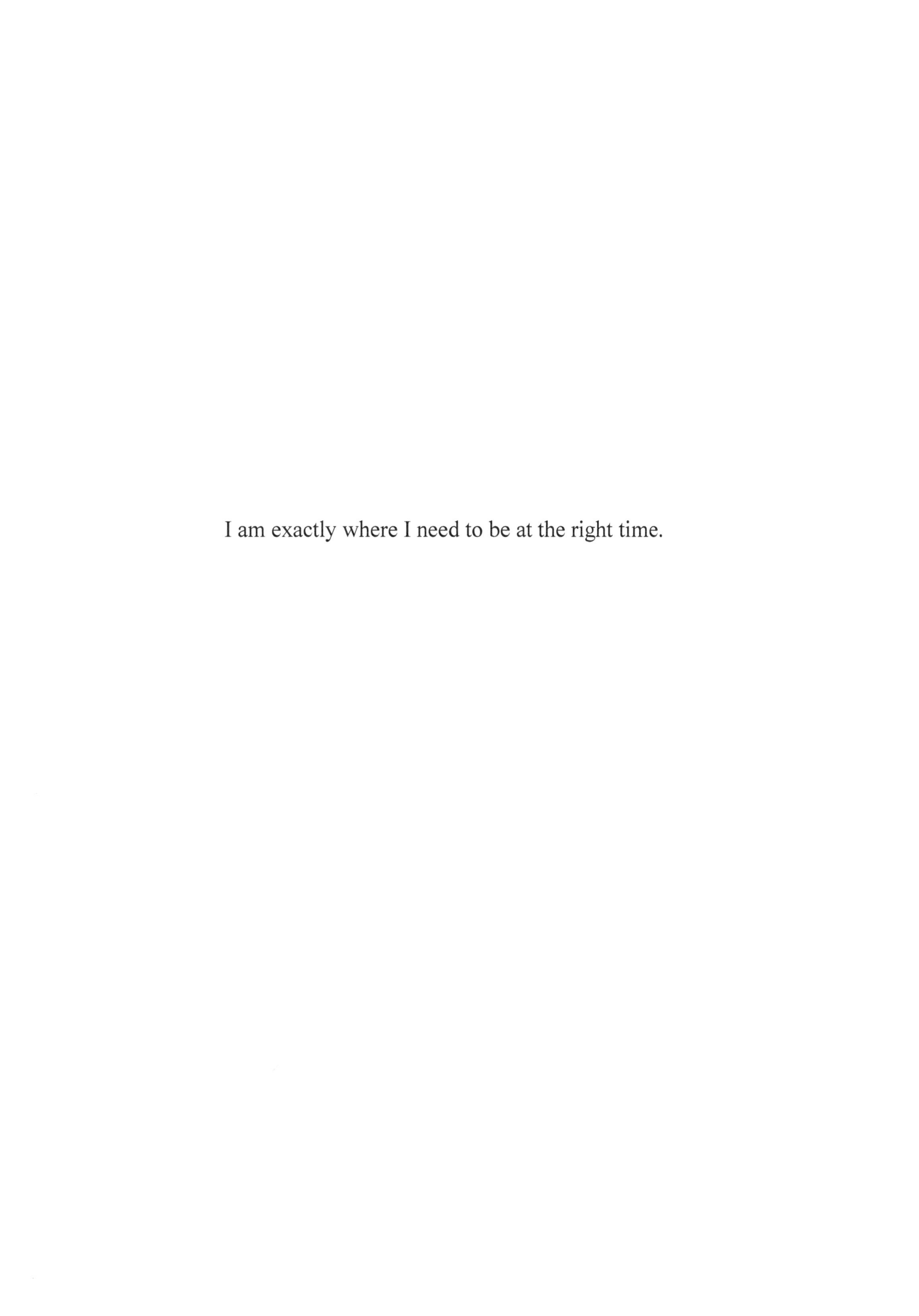

I am exactly where I need to be at the right time.

How can I be, do, and have...

even better today?

I improve myself every day.

I also give myself time to rest, play, love,

and give myself self care.

I ask myself

better and better questions

every day

and

get better and better answers

every day.

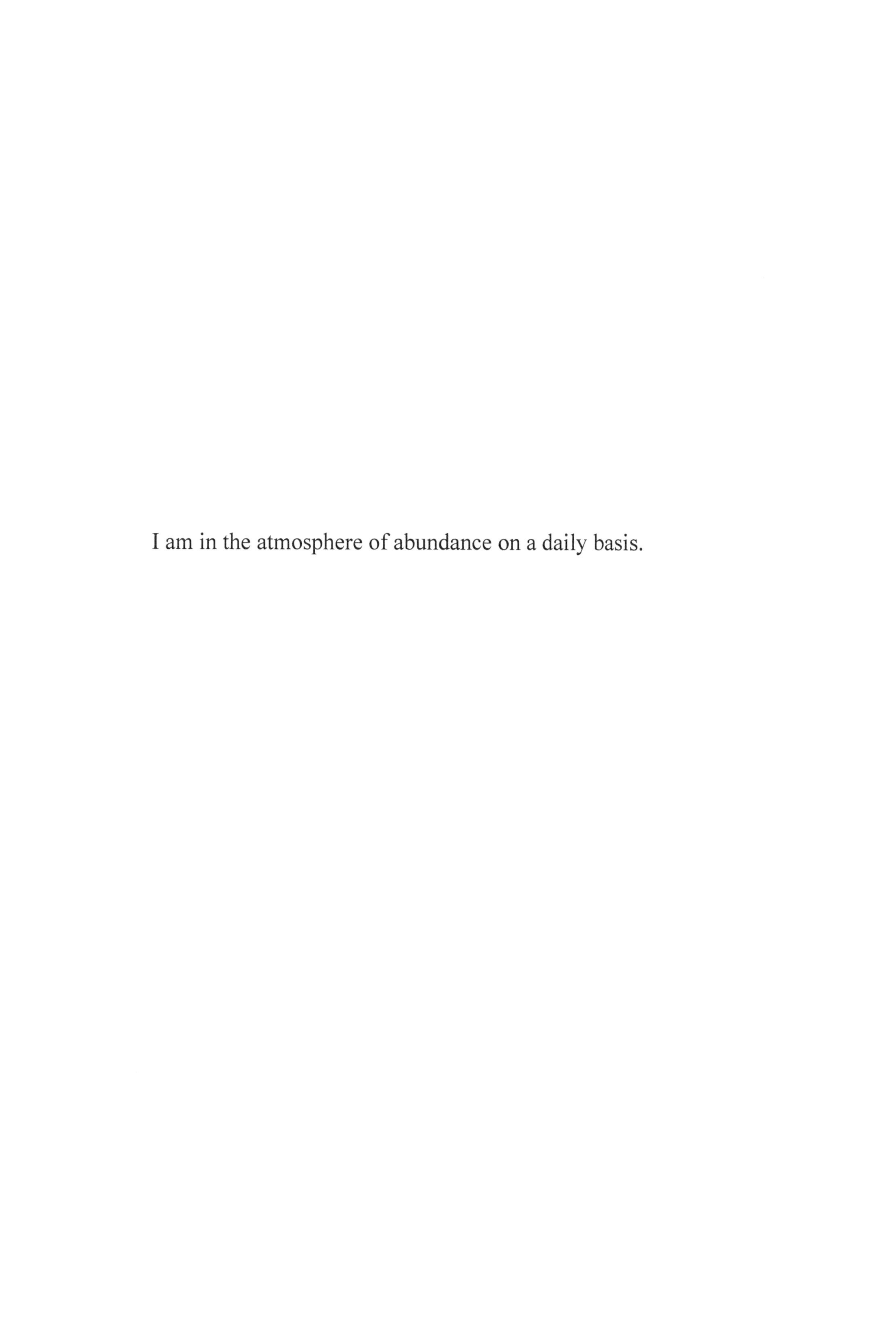

I am in the atmosphere of abundance on a daily basis.

I fear not.

I am one with success.

I know that when I have a plan,

everything in

my life becomes simpler.

What is success for me?

I allow the answers to come

even if they are different

than what I imagined.

Happiness is success.

What is success for me?

I allow the answer

to be better than

anything that I

have ever imagined.

I live a balanced and joyful life.

I am progressing towards my goal

more and more, every day.

I control my inner game in order to

succeed at my outer game.

I believe there is always a loving and

guided way to achieve the success I seek.

I start my brand new life today

with joy and ease,

love and fulfillment.

My life works for me more and more,

better and better…everyday, all of the time.

I build the momentum needed

by creating consistent routines

that help me move towards my goal.

Everything,

in every way,

is always working out for me.

I am moving forward

with great ease

and great success.

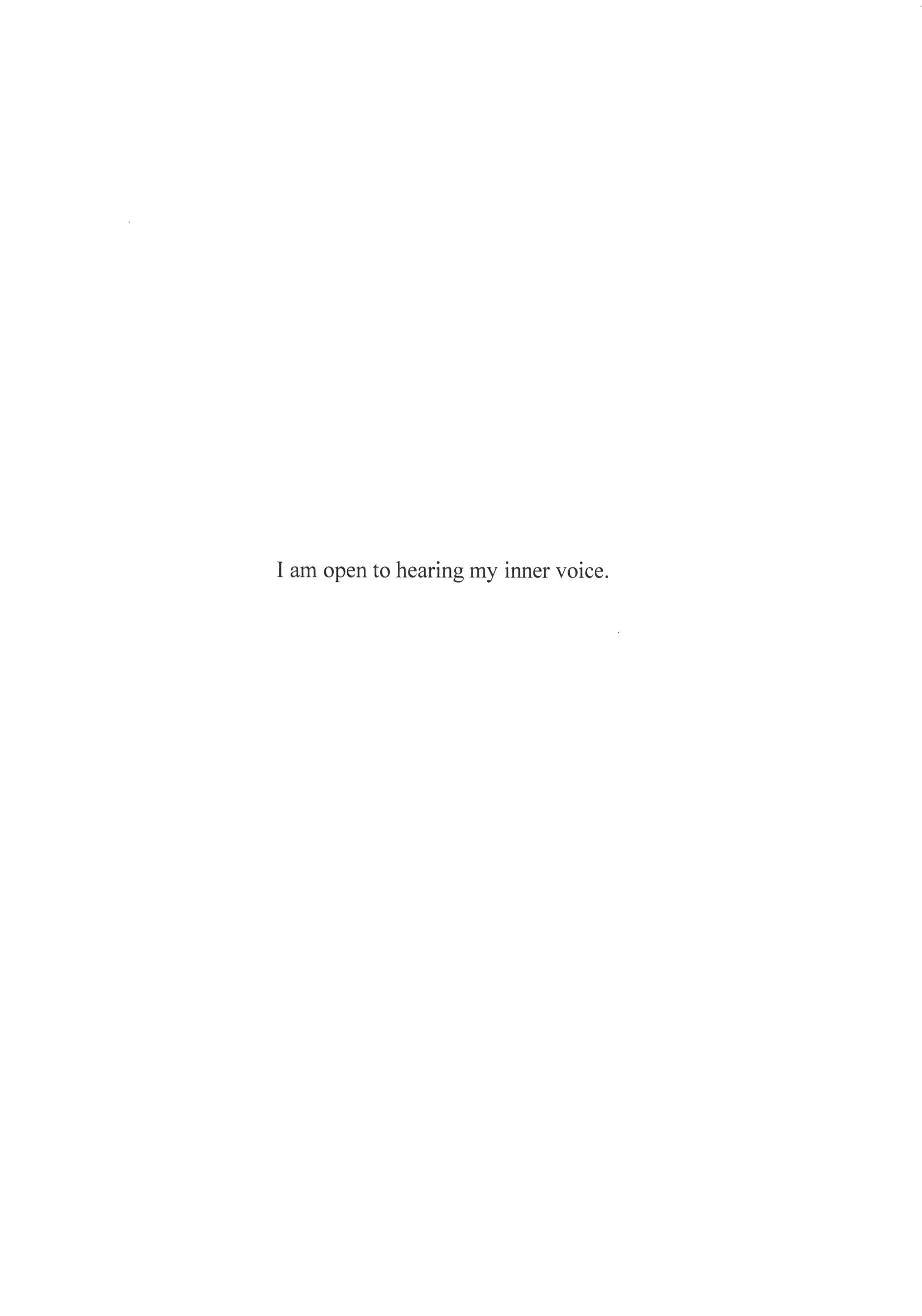

I am open to hearing my inner voice.

It's happening for me! My life is

showing me signs that I'm doing the right

things at the right time,

and steadily moving towards my goal.

I focus on all the things that

matter to me in my life.

I remove the idea of perfectionism,

and let my humanness shine.

The meaning I hold for my

success may have changed,

and that is all right.

Universe,

thank you for guiding

me to what is next.

I love who I am in this moment.

I love where I am in this moment.

I accept what I am becoming

in this moment.

I have a clear plan for my life in every category.

I have a great attitude and my results reflect it.

I have created a target and

I put my efforts towards it

with a clear plan.

I am flexible.

I am accountable.

Sure! I would love to.

I keep telling a new and better story

every day, and my

life keeps getting better.

Success is here for me now.

Life keeps working out for me

in such amazing ways.

The power and consistency of my desire is

lighting up

the path of least resistance for me.

There's always another answer.

There's always a better answer.

How I get there is by asking

better and better questions.

Everything is working out for me

better than

I could ever have imagined.

I expect the very best

and therefore

receive the very best.

I am a winner.

I feel like a winner.

I act like a winner.

I experience winning results.

I take the time to set goals in every area of my life.

Everyday I take the time to review my goals,

update them, note when there

is movement towards

them, and give thanks.

I have a grateful heart.

I make it a practice to become

aware of any and

all internal resistance

that block my intention.

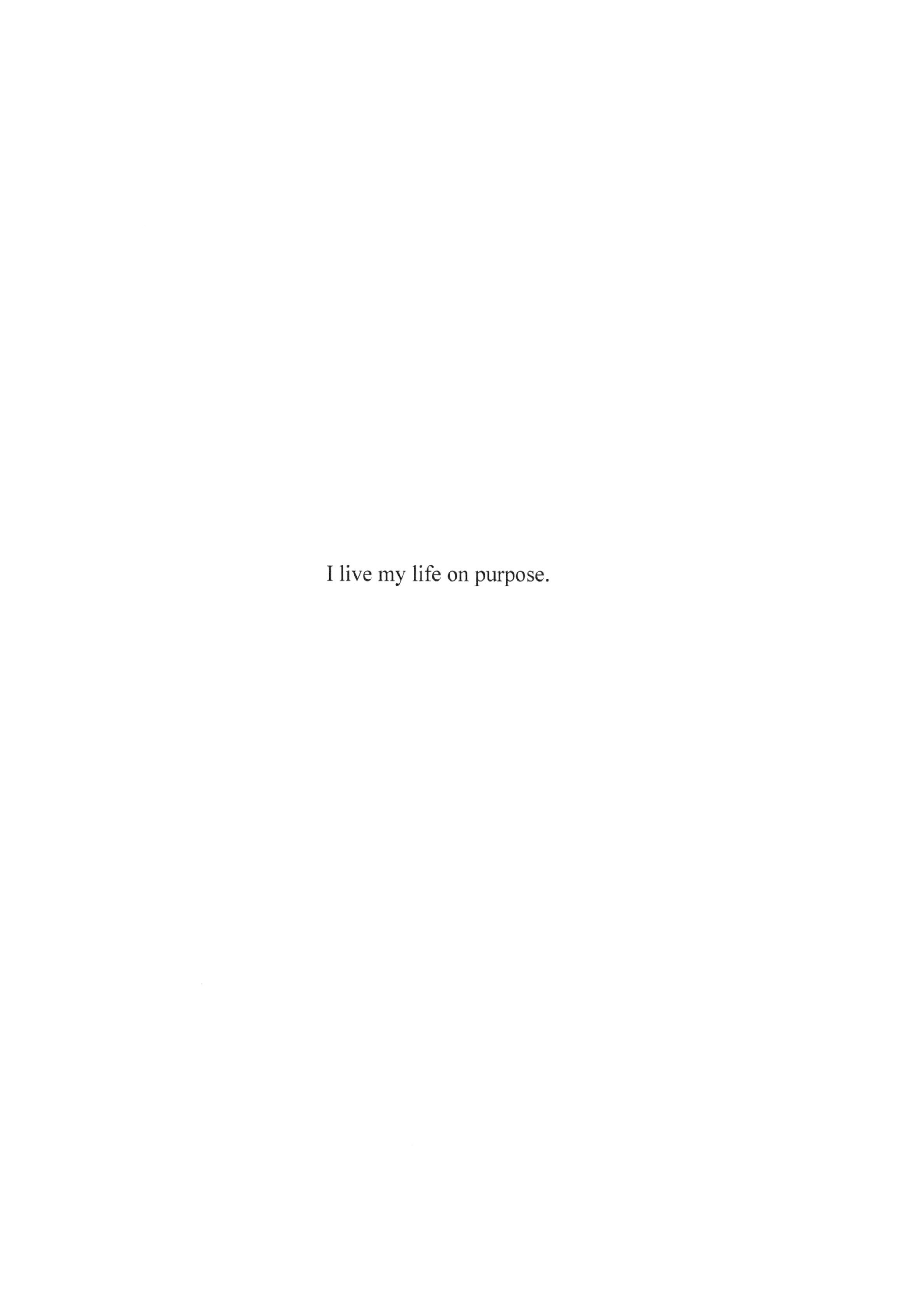

I live my life on purpose.

I know how precious this life is and how lucky

I am to have an opportunity to do my

very best, give my very best,

and live my very best life.

I feel so grateful for all

the good things in my life.

I feel grateful for all of the people,

places and things in my life

that help to make it better.

I feel the joy, joy, joy, joy, down in my heart.

I realize how important it is that I

stay in the energy of happy.

When I love others,

I am loved.

I have a generous heart.

When I appreciate others,

I am appreciated.

I take the time I need to make sure

that I am healthy

and

that my relationships are a priority

because I know that

balance is the key to a great life.

I am happy to take time out

of every day to

visualize and

imagine my intentions

and desires.

I connect my emotions with a

joy of experiencing

and succeeding.

I affirm that I am worth it.

I affirm that I am worthy.

I affirm that I have value.

I do everything I can

to be so valuable

that I cannot be ignored.

What if I knew that every "i" was dotted

and every "*t*" was crossed

and that I was definitely on my way

to achieving my dreams?

I am clear on my end goals.

I give thanks for everything

that happens in my day that

moves me towards my goal.

I make sure that I am always learning

and always growing.

I am happy to help others

towards their success as

I work towards my own.

When I have doubts, I take the time to

understand what those doubts are

so that I can move forward.

I listen to myself think.

I listen to myself speak.

I observe instances

of lack and limitation.

I replace them with

positive and affirming language.

I face my fears.

I do the very best I can and

ask for help when I need it.

I do my best to show up

100% for myself each day.

But when I don't, I give myself

grace and try again tomorrow.

I'm proud of myself

for showing up and

doing what I need to do

in order to achieve the goal/s

I set for myself today.

I am successful.

I am happy.

I am confident.

I am focused on

the outcome!

I invite the people into my life

who will help me move to the next level.

I'm completely open to how my intention unfolds.

I am unphased by the difficulty of the project,

knowing that I will rise to the occasion

and grow myself to be bigger

than any difficulty I face.

I am aligned with my abundance.

I am always looking for the signs

that show me which direction I need to go.

I align with the happiest and best results.

I know whatever I believe, I can achieve.

I take the time each day to center myself

and understand any resistance,

fear, lack and limitation thinking.

I do what is necessary to turn it around

so that I am on the road to a

joyous and successful outcome.

I have decided what I want

and I do not waver.

The momentum of my journey

is strong and the alignment to

my desire is expected.

On a daily basis I condition

my mind and emotional

set points for wealth and success.

Whatever I focus on consistently

I get more of, so I make sure

I'm focused on what I want,

NOT what I don't.

It is that easy. It is that simple.

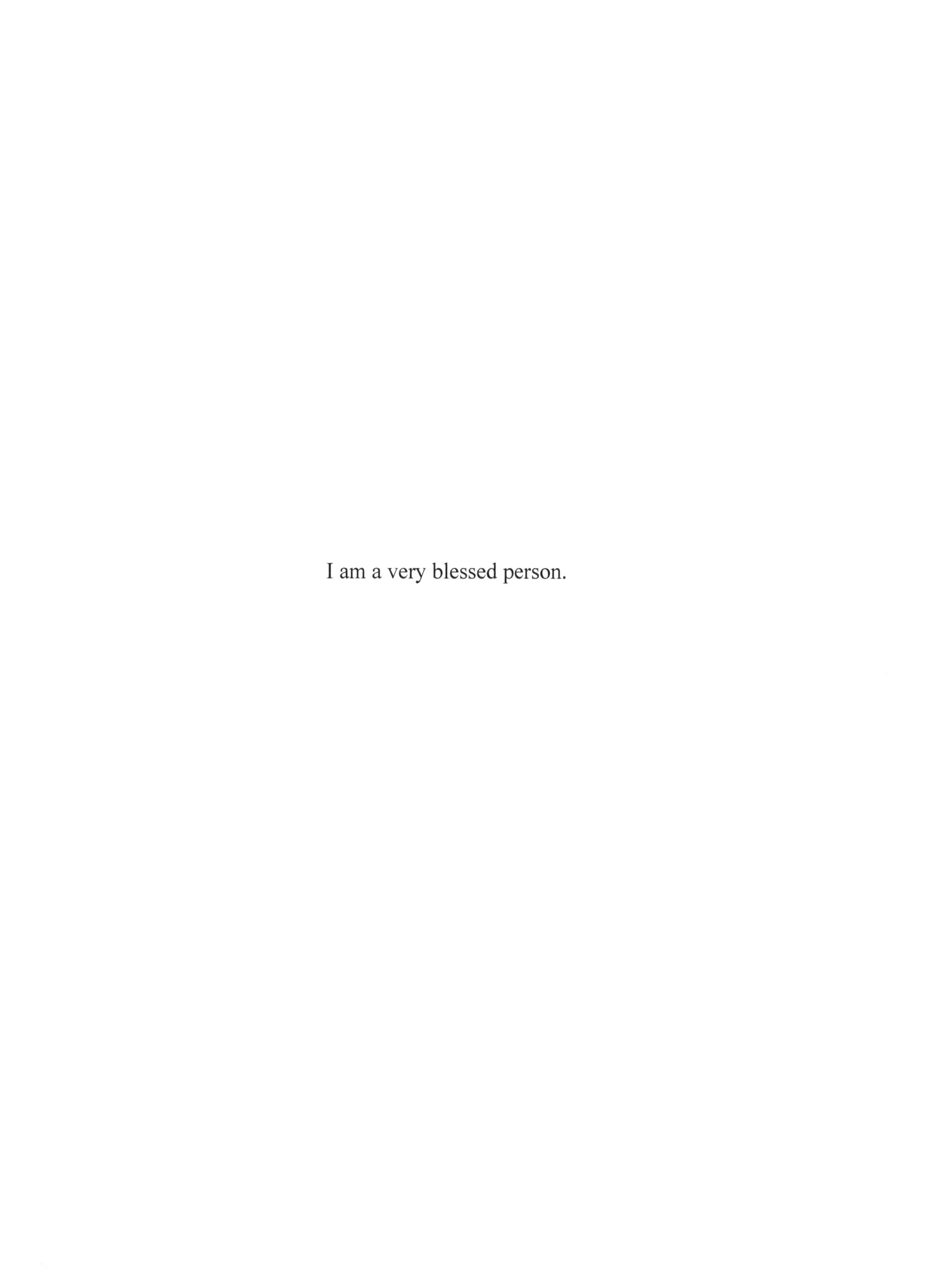
I am a very blessed person.

I am grateful for

this moment,

this day...this life.

I give thanks for all of the

blessings that are destined

to unfold in my favor.

Everyday,

I meditate on my desired income

(both passive and earned),

believing.

I am willing to change and allow the results.

I am mindful of my money

and make sure that

I pay myself first,

invest in myself,

and begin to grow my money

in a way that works best for me.

I know that passive income

is my route to financial freedom

and financial success.

I know that if I don't have it yet

the results will come in

perfect timing, in perfect ways.

I believe I can allow this truth into

my awareness and conscious mind.

This belief works to change my mindset,

conditioning, as well as

mental and emotional blocks.

I have made a list of the things

that I intend to achieve

and look at that list daily,

knowing that I am on path

to my alignment and realization.

All that I desire is done.

All is well.

I release the energy of my desires

to my higher self

and the wisdom of the Universe.

I know that the success

I seek is showing me how to receive it.

I'm a very blessed person.

Blessings follow me wherever I go.

I make it a point to live in a

"focus bubble"

where I only allow

words, images, thoughts,

and people that support

my success, intentions, and dreams.

THE POWER OF GRATITUDE

"When I started counting my blessings,

my whole life turned around."

Willie Nelson

AN ATTITUDE OF GRATITUDE

The metaphysics of being grateful is that it can positively impact your reality if you make it a daily practice. It is a great focusing tool and being grateful carries with it a high vibrational energy that can attract positive experiences and opportunities as you go on the journey towards whatever goal you have set out to achieve. Gratitude can shift your focus from worry, fear, and thinking about what is not working in your life to a focus of the things that are working, even if it isn't that much to begin with. This one act can create a sense of abundance and contentment. A shift in focus also helps you realize and appreciate the good things in life right now. It helps build your awareness so that you can continue to confirm and affirm the even better things that will begin to come because of the consistent work you are doing towards your goal.

As you start to experience increased feelings of happiness and satisfaction your vibration raises and you will start to align with more and better things. Gratitude is a powerful energy and by cultivating a practice of it you can positively impact your progress as you do the other work needed to create a more fulfilling and joyful life. I have given you some gratitude affirmations to get you started and highly recommend that you also create gratitude affirmations of you own that resonate with you and reflect the increasing blessings in your life.

I have a lot to be grateful for.

I live my life with an attitude of gratitude.

I am so grateful that the past

doesn't have to dictate my future.

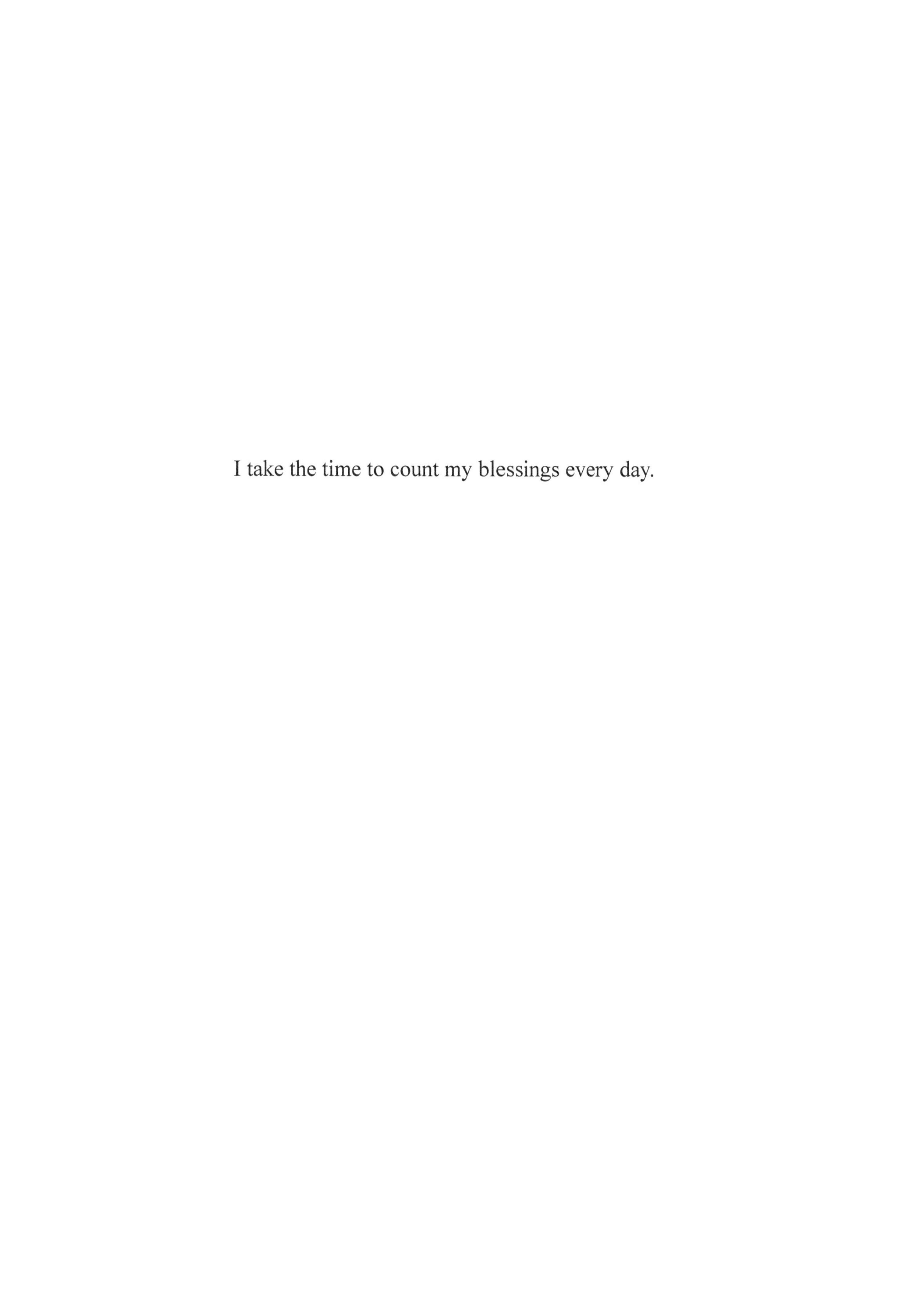

I take the time to count my blessings every day.

I am so grateful for all of

the blessings of my life.

I am so grateful that my life has meaning.

I am thankful that I feel like I have purpose.

I am so grateful for my health,

wealth, and the love in my life.

I am so grateful that my family

is happy and healthy.

I am so thankful that the changes that

are happening now are for my ultimate good.

I am grateful that the success

I have achieved is fulfilling,

and that I continue to grow and do

better and better every day.

I appreciate the process.

Every day I am finding more things

to be grateful for.

I remind myself each day how

blessed I am and how grateful

I am for all of the good that

keeps coming my way.

"You are your best thing."

Toni Morrison

ABOUT THE AUTHOR

Sheree L. Ross is an award winning writer and a student of metaphysics. She is an entrepreneur and investor in real estate, fashion, food, and film, alongside a 25 year career in the fashion industry. In the early aughts she created the popular fashion blog Preppybaba for masculine of center fashion lovers. Sheree is a wealth literacy activist with the vision of generational wealth for POC and LGBTQ communities. She is passionate about people and understands that we are all here to live our very best lives and love the lives that we live. She understands that emotions, thoughts, focus, conditioning, and core beliefs are the keys to our outer joy and the life that we wish to experience. She brings experience from years as a metaphysical student and entrepreneur to help push thought beyond perceived limitations. Sheree focuses on visionary leadership around creative culture, visionary expression, and the infinite possibilities that lay within each one of us..